BLACK LIVES MATTER Special Ezine					August 2020

©LOUD & QUEER 2020					Marisa Wohlschlaeger

BLACK LIVES MATTER Special Ezine   August 2020

BLACK LIVES MATTER
SPECIAL EZINE

©LOUD & QUEER 2020   Marisa Wohlschlaeger

CONTENTS

What is the Okra Project?	1
Lorenzo Buford— Not your negro or a fixed constellation, Trans Obituary, Not Yours, & Winter America [1,2]	2-6
Maurice Moore—The Tradition, Hands Up Don't Shoot!, Token, Legendary Children	7-10
Mike Andrews, aka Prometheus— Leaves, My Energy, Say What You Want, Ripped Open [1,2]	11-14
Aquarius Funkk—Femme Masked: An Exploration of Performing Femininity	15-23
Teddy Alexis Rodriguez—Chosen Family [2,3]	24-37
Milicent Fambrough— Love, Shape	38-39
Spencer Millington— Tides, Sunflowers, New Intensity	40-42
Elijah Nicholas— Madoodle	43-44
Become a Patron	45

Content Warning Legend

[1] Violence [2] Explicit Language [3] Sexual Language

LOUD & QUEER   CW: None

What is the Okra Project?

The Okra Project is a collective that seeks to address the global crisis faced by Black Trans people by bringing home cooked, healthy, and culturally specific meals and resources to Black Trans People wherever we can reach them.

During the Middle Passage, our African ancestors snuck okra onto captive ships to sustain themselves and plant in the new world. Black Diasporic cooking traditions often use the okra plant for its versatility and it is often associated with health, prosperity, and community.

In this spirit, The Okra Project hopes to extend free, delicious, and nutritious meals to Black Trans people experiencing food insecurity.

How Does it Work?

It's actually very simple! Based on individual donations, The Okra Project pays Black Trans chefs to go into the homes of Black Trans people to cook them a healthy and home-cooked meal at **absolutely no cost to our Black TGNC siblings**. For those Black Trans folks currently experiencing homeless or whose homes cannot support our chef's cooking, The Okra Project has partnered with institutions like Osborne Association and other community spaces to deliver foods.

One Session Costs The Okra Project $90
(Including Chef Pay & Groceries)

To Make That Possible:
  18 people could donate $5
  9 people could donate $10
  6 people could donate $15
  3 people could donate $30
  1 super generous human could donate $90

Visit their website to donate
https://www.flipcause.com/hosted_widget/hostedWidgetHome/MTAxMzk3

LOUD & QUEER　　　　　　　　　　　　　　CW: Violence, Explicit Language

Not a fixed negro or constellation
Lorenzo Buford

for your viewing pleasures.
Not a dispirited location to building housing
and flight is not in captivity.

Will not succumb to riots in the corral.
Not violently waiting for your permissions.
Am claustrophobic in the time-oriented flesh.

My skin color will bring the demise
of debilitating gods.
Will twist their fishing poles into
noose to hang their mask
of insanity that hides their hideousness.

Not decimated in expulsions
from their imagined entitlement
even as their images become specks in my eyes
that weep so perception is
not distorted and their voices
will not peel off the skin color.

Will not wash their sins out
of my blackness as I walk
exiled in their cities
slowly disappearing from consciousness.
Inner flood waters will not
be putting out this fire making wings.

My skin color cocoons.
Interlopers' monuments crumble.
The cocoon writhes with a damnation fire...
that has not yet emerged

and this skin is not a ticket.
The goodness of society curses this skin
when it cannot desexualize,
dehumanize and decapitate.

Others will taste the bitter waters
in their mouth speaking of my rage
when I am not the goodness to
be paraded and marketed as a good slave.

The skin color will not
sustain a world of the living dead
and be its ghost to sanction its madness.

Letting go of the reins of the ghost, the slave.
Will not be an echo, a remnant of what was
but let go of skin color to be - *what is to be*.

Not human when dying into
the mouth of a masked devourer.

So, the dehumanized becomes a reminder
humans are not the staging ground
just a place of cleansing others' excrements.

Trans Obituary

(In memoriam for a murdered trans woman)

"Pay attention to my body,"
says a trans woman.
"Not a boy in a dress.
Do not paint my face as acceptable
to matrix media.
Did not hear me alive
and still deny me dead.
Do not disfigure my potential.
Brutality is not a work of art.
I am not a fake woman!"

"Do not paint my old life as acceptable
for a colonizing media.
Did not ask for this finale, a brutal exit,
by a rage of hatred."

A political plate is passed
to serve my mind,
my heart, my body, my color.
Thought it would be old age quietness,
laughing at memories.

I am welcomed by the murdered
trans women who are comforters
from the violence inflicted,
who wash off the tainted blood,
the hurt, the crazy,
the lamenting, the shouting.

"Do not kill me! I want to live,"
I said with swollen eyes.
I will not give the perpetrator
a voice and image inside my heaven.

"Pay attention to my realness," says a trans woman.
"My heart says I am trans woman
and those who find this dead body
say this is a man without purpose,
a man who is lost; a confused one
as they shuffle their laughter
behind their political voice
and their upturned eyes judge.

I see them from a place
they cannot go because
my god does not like ugly
especially when others
make thought forms to masquerade
as a god that loves straight life only
and not the Other,
the fringe dweller, the outcast.

Pay attention as you put away this body.
Discard me not in a news item marked
'Not important'. I know I will look back
with a comforting hand when another
trans woman is marked as a *finale* before her time.

Voices of trans women murdered before
call out as psycho pomps.
I see them. I will walk with them.
Sometimes an angel has a tragic path
so, you can find the voice of the heart
to give you breath,
to give you compassion; to awaken
the dead inside...back to life.

LOUD & QUEER   CW: Violence, Explicit Language

Not Yours

Not your Negro. Not your boy.
Not your Black. Not your nigger.
Not your colored…not….

Slave names attempt to
appropriate soul expressions
and attempt to dehydrate
while castrating the mind
to arrest self-awareness
to creates blockages
while walking roads of consciousness.

But you learn to shed
the names of the oppressors,
the gender restrictions of the colonizers
and the artificial needs of a predator.

There will be no curfew
for an ancestral voice, a remnant voice,
an Osirian voice
because the names of oppressions
will have no validity
nor allow one to be named
as a beast in the artificial gardens.

Not yours. Not yours. Not yours.

About the author
Lorenzo Neal Buford is a poet, a fiction writer, a playwright, songwriter/performer.
Visit author's website: www.LorenzoBuford.com

Visit youtube page: https://www.youtube.com/user/LorenzoBuford

Email: Lorenzo.buford@gmail.com

New works arriving in August 2020 – The Monstrous Soul Poetry Series

Winter America

Diseased winds carry parasitic thoughts
that escape from mouths
speaking dead words.
and inhaling the fumes of colonization
from breathing in the chemically infused air
which is accelerating
the fragmenting of consciousness
so, outside frequencies can make islands in the mind,
bring a consuming fire
in rooms of the mind now for rent
to make ghosts from images, narratives within
that drink fallen angels now thoughtforms.

The web of lies continue to strangle
citizens into blind submission.
An orange clown with poison balloon words
permeates the sightline of gazes
as people consume and become
addicts divided in their perception.

The plague spreads across a world
burning a fire within that is unholy
and making cracks in the soil
so, the ghosts denied rises.

Consumption of the weak within
is heralding the time of demons.
Winter America - in the speech of the sheep -
is quietly being herded
into an extinction event
so, the land can be fertilized
for colonization and consumption
by foreign installations.

The harvest is being sauced
to thwart the perpetual slaves
from rising as suns.

A fever crawls through the consciousness
like an uncontrollable fire
as people's fears fuel the virus' consumption.

As coldness overlays most,
there is a gaze of predatory survival.
Feasting demons sit in the background
waiting for waiters to bring their entrée.

The Tradition
Maurice Moore

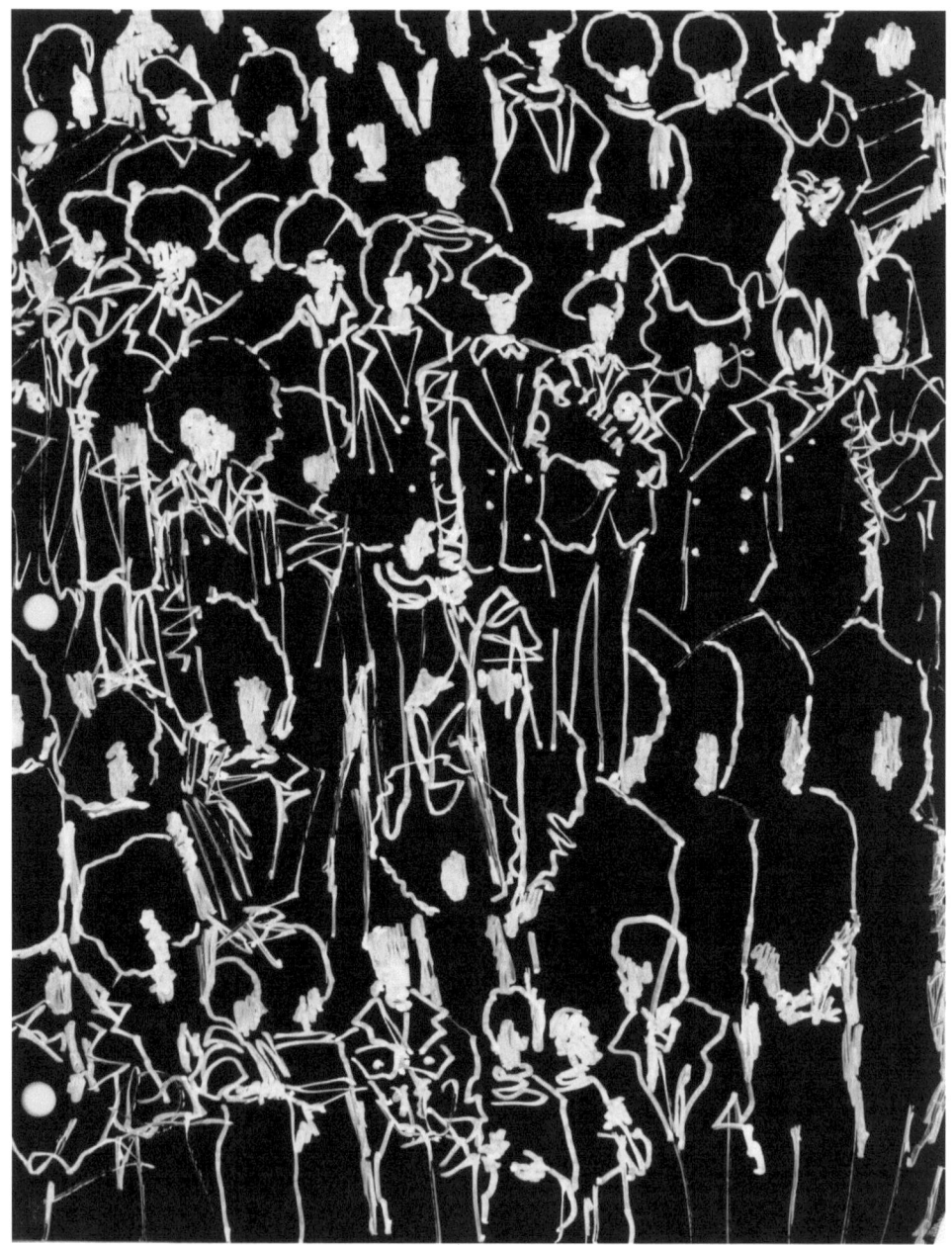

LOUD & QUEER   CW: None

Hands Up Don't Shoot!

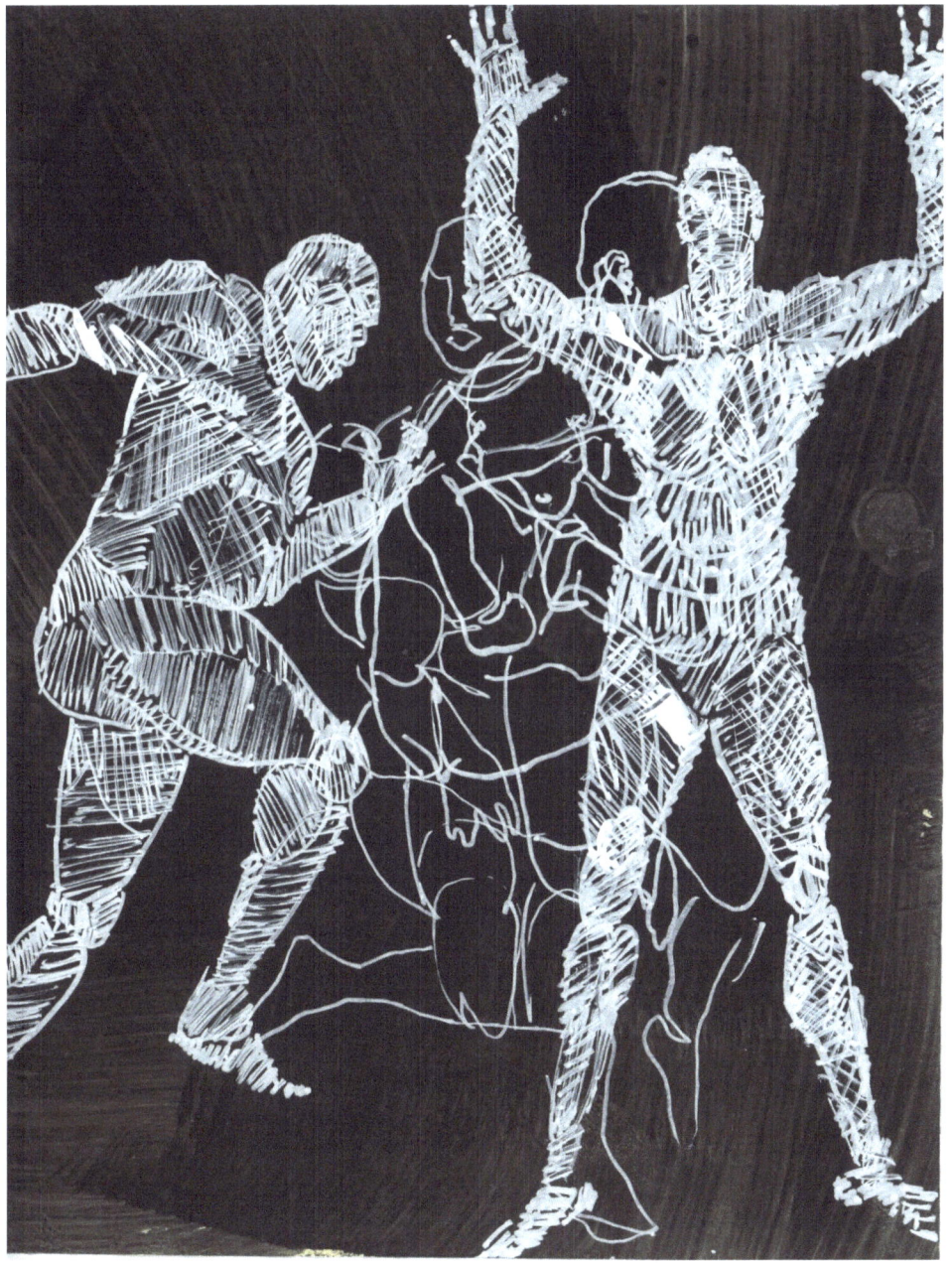

Token

I notice when I'm the only one in the room.

.

Legendary Children

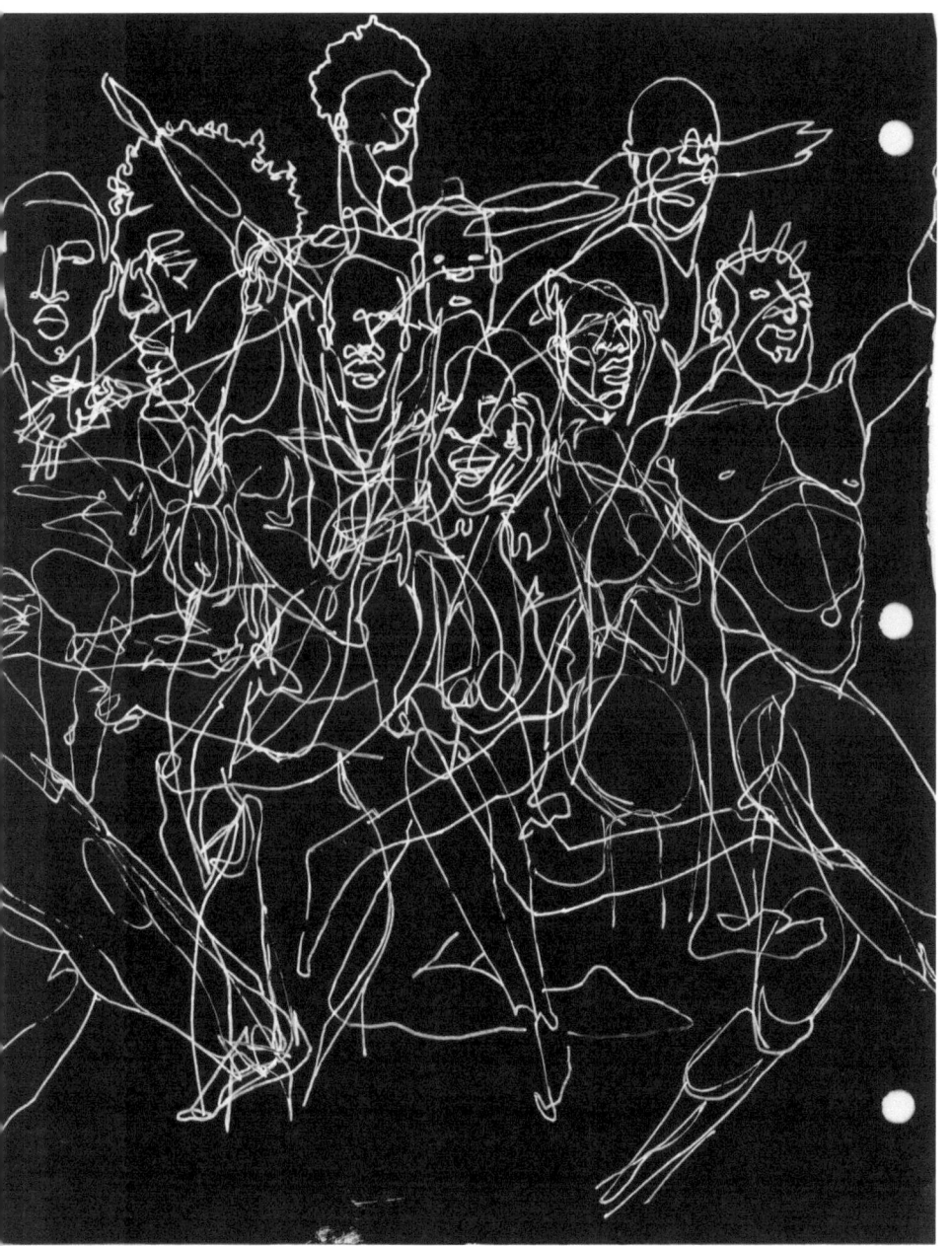

Leaves
Mike Andrews aka Prometheus

As I walked through this forest
I saw all of these trees that were fallen
Do trees care about other trees?
Or do they just fall and make a noise that no one hears?
We make noise, too
But does anyone hear us?
Do we turn our backs whenever we can't stand the noise?
There's truth in noise
I passed the caves and the rocks and the streams
The water bubbled as I stared into the clear drink
Fish here and there, darting, feeding, mating....
They follow the path written up for them
But do we fall under the same categories?
We have free will.
We can listen. We can ignore. We can fight
We can have opposing views
I crunched my way up a hill, as the ground inclined
Leaves under my feet, they crackled and gave way
To my weight
Animals big and small
They know the cold has come
They gather food to survive the harsh months to come
Like the months we go through, maybe just days or years
Depending on our roads
I saw the sun, it went down, but the upper half still remained
Peeking over the top of the hill
Like a toddler's head, peeking over the counter
Looking at the cookies
That's the way it crumbles
We hear everyone say
Protect your cookies, folks
The cabin was where I was told it would be
Dark and brooding it may have been
I was going to enjoy the quiet
My reflections of the world overlooking my usual thoughts
Like the shelter I found in this house
Made of wood
From the trees
That once had leaves
That overlooks the valley
Is there peace down there?

My Energy

Channeling my energy into the aspects of my life that matter to me, make me smile, make me cry, but tears of joy.
Channeling my energy into true relationships
Both friends and family as well.
Channeling my energy into helping others, even if we're not in the same circle
That's what compassion is
We can't all be friends, but respect me and I'll return the favor
Channeling my energy into goals that I'm working on, regardless of the amount of applause, or lack thereof
Even though I work twice as hard to get half as far.
Channeling my energy into love, life, and happiness,
Life is too short to be upset all the time
I've learned over time
Channeling my energy into what and whom uplifts and empowers me
Fake support has no place here
It should be mutual and genuine.
Channeling my energy into becoming a better person as I'm not perfect
I'm just me.
Channeling my energy into caring for others Without taking from myself
Because I can be passionate
Even though I sometimes have a funny way of Showing it.
Channeling my energy into my art, my creativity, and the magic that makes up a part Of who I am.
No longer wasting, no longer investing my Energy into "maybes" and "we'll sees"
But investing in actions
Show me and I'll show you.
Our energies may not match
It's human nature
But it's also a beautiful thing
As we all are different.

LOUD & QUEER   CW: Violence, Explicit Language

Say What You Want

I'm still here,
I'm still queer
Yes, you're right....
Get used to it
I am black.
My skin is brown
I will be who I want
I won't satisfy your
Stupid perceptions
Media has had a hand
In perpetrating
No, I am not
MUSCLED UP
RICH
MASCULINE
Where's it say that?
Where's the scrolls
This shit was scribbled on?
Do I HAVE to be the way you want?
Do I NEED to act out your
Fucked up fantasies.....
In order to
JUSTIFY
Your bias?
Your blindness?
Become a bandwagon bitch
Jump on and do what others are doing
Don't judge for yourself
Don't believe the facts
But don't open your mouth
Don't spread the LIES!

About the author
I am a 40 year old gender queer Black man. My pronouns are he, him, his, they, them, theirs. I run a GLBTQ+ Arts & Literary Project called FLAME!, which was started in 2015 and I'm based out of Boston, Massachusetts. I will be relaunching my arts and literary journal this year. I have been writing since grade school and hope to publish my first collection of poetry soon.

My links are: facebook.com/artsjournalonfire
IG: flame_glbtq
Website (which is still undergoing changes): creativeflame.squarespace.com

Ripped Open

It bleeds, it's sore
I can't feel anything more
my soul's been ripped open
and I'm empty to the core...
the trees in the forest have swayed back and forth
as I walked through and pondered their worth
they're bending, I thought
but they're supposed to be strong
tall and mighty, for so many years long
I guess they have suffered
the same fate I have, weak, but not broken
they bleed, they're sore
they can't feel anymore
their souls have been ripped open
and they're empty to the core
the child that plays
with his little toy train
cries and weeps
because of the pain
he sees his mom, hurt by the man
who is supposed to be dad
their lives in shambles,
the worst few years he has ever had
he wants to intervene, but he has no spirit left
it bleeds, it's sore,
he can't feel anything more
his tears are full, but he's empty inside
his soul's been ripped open
he's empty to the core....
my life, my love, my happiness and joy
I can not seem to live without
the sun has gone down,
and it's dark within my heart
all the mean and the bad and the shady
have come and done their part
but I have found a way to get back what's mine
my soul will be mended
and that sun will once again shine
no more ripped souls
no more bleeding, nor being sore
I have overcome my weakness
and I hurt no more.....
the trees will stand strong against the wind
the child will play with smiles again
and I will walk into the morning sun

Femme Masked: An Exploration of Performing Femininity
Aquarius Funkk

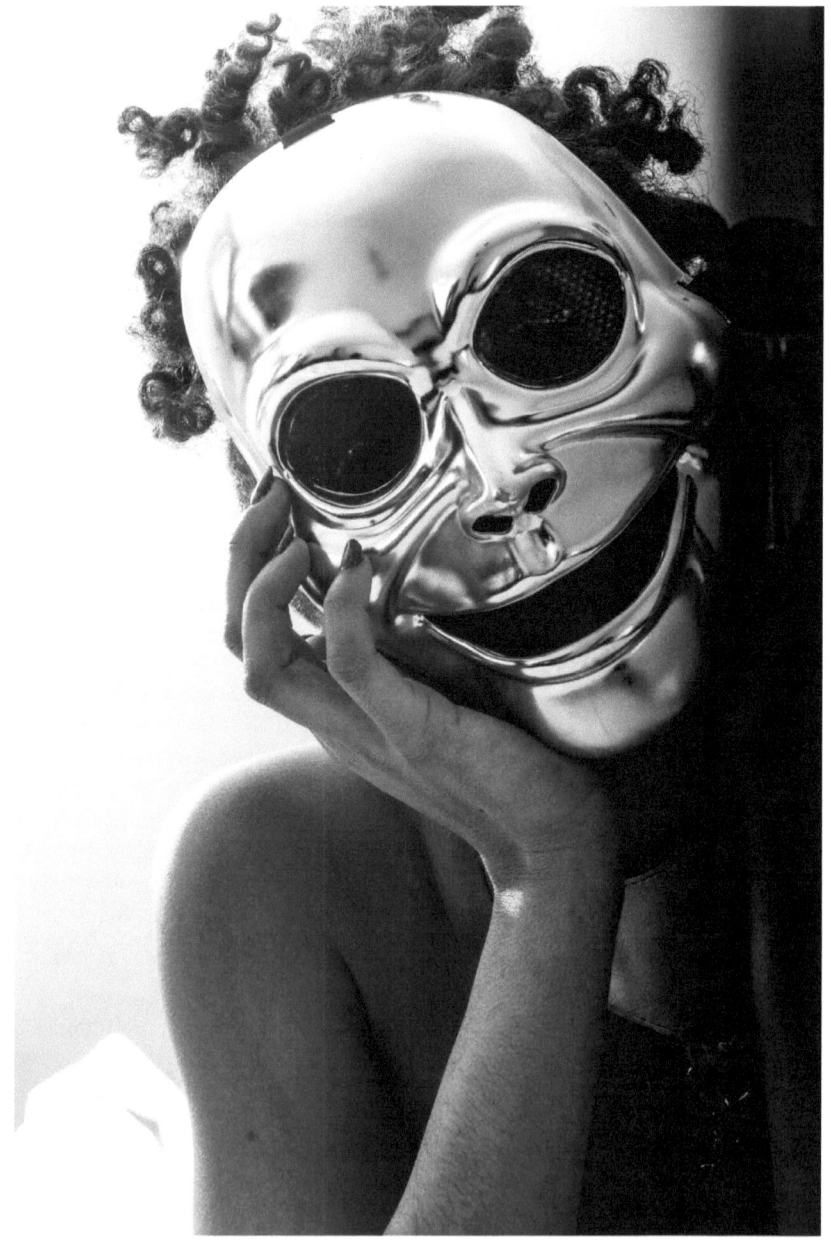

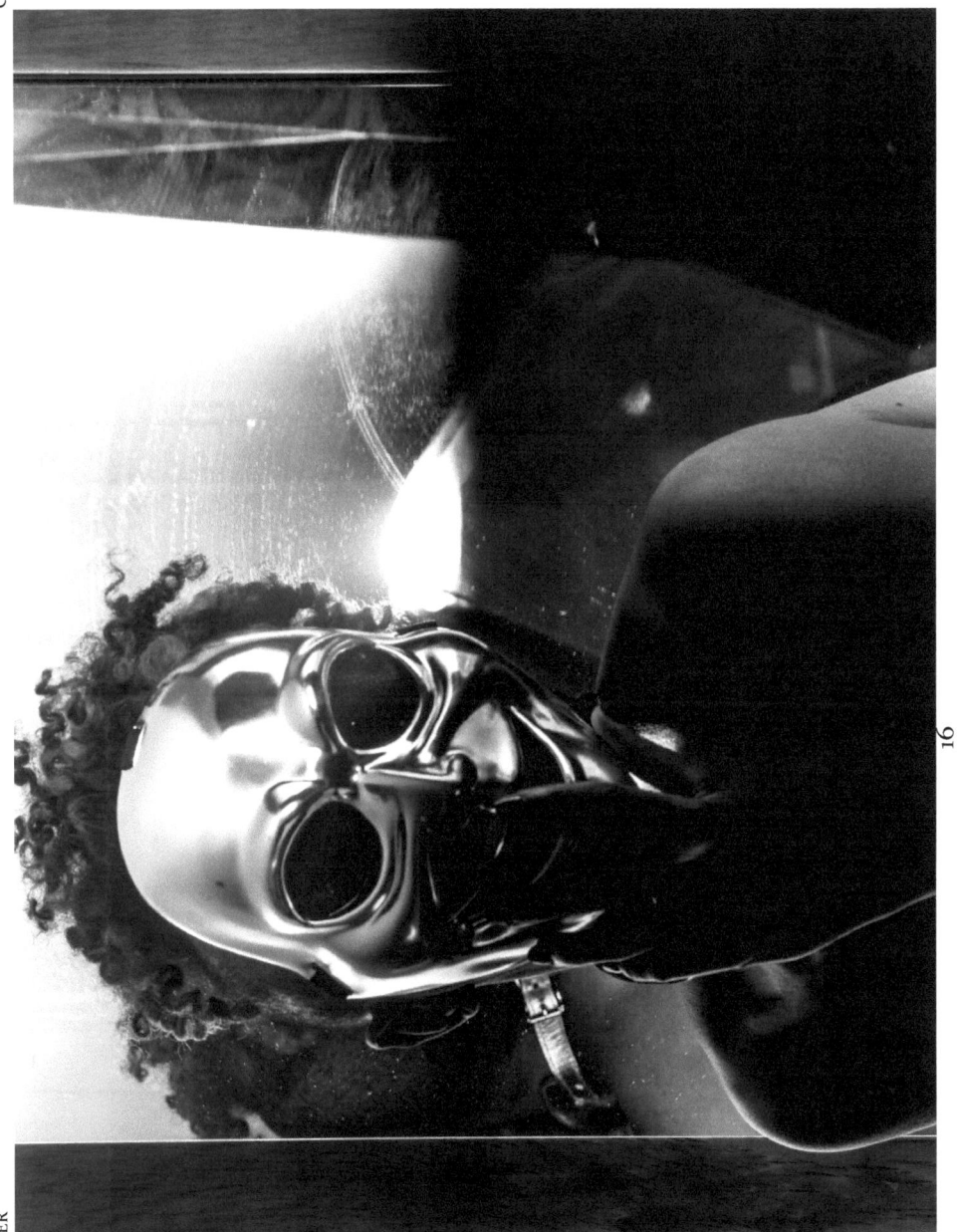

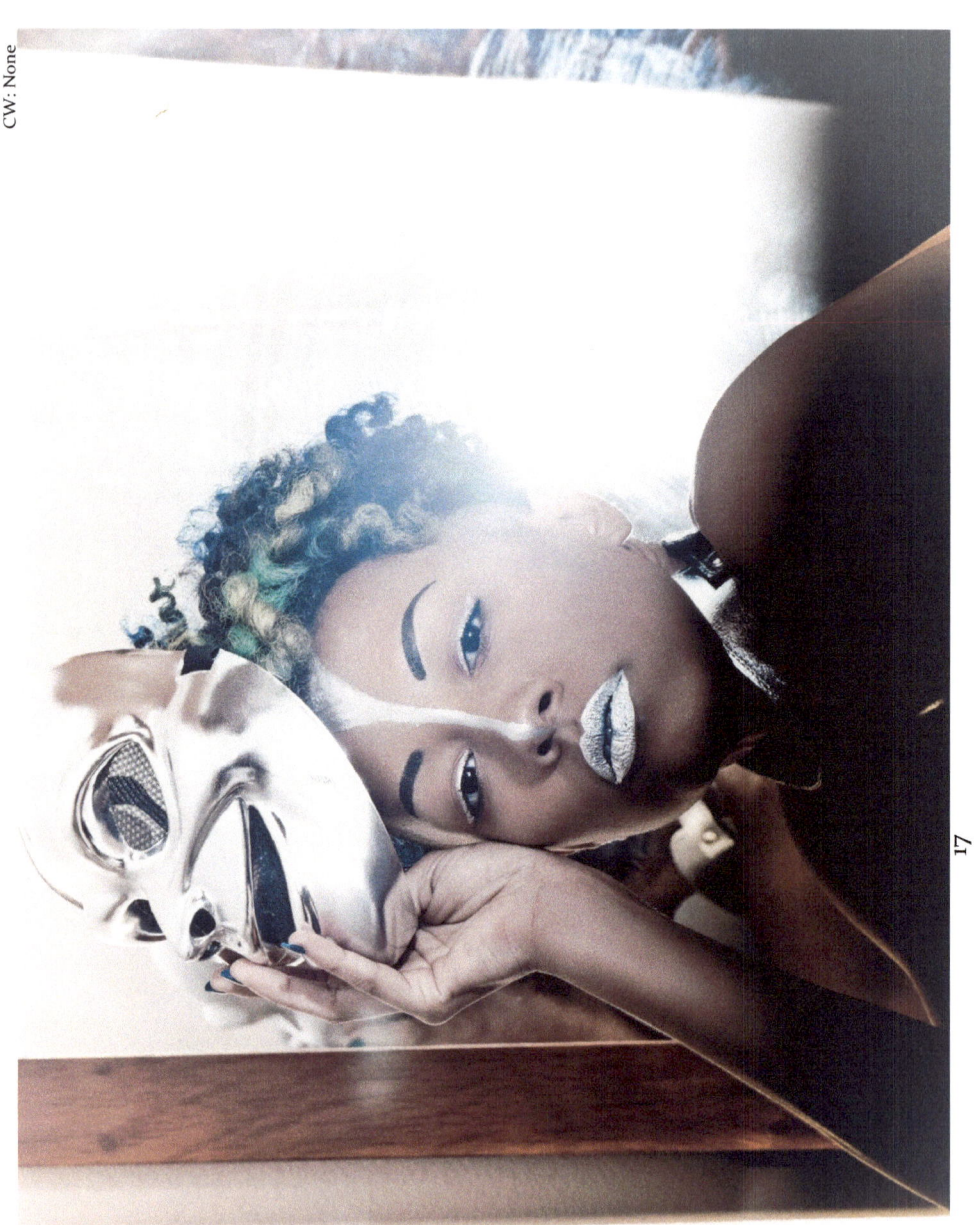

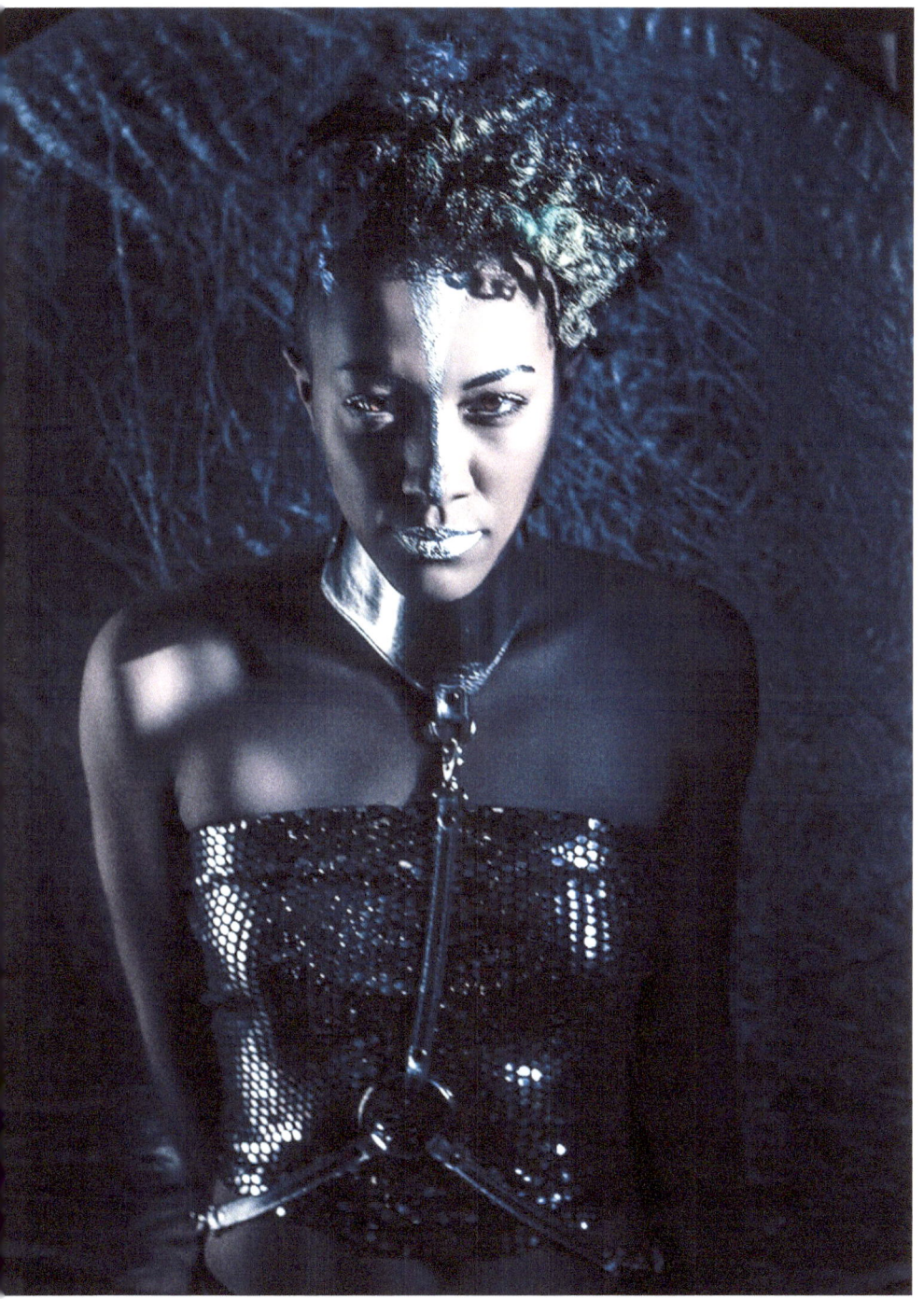

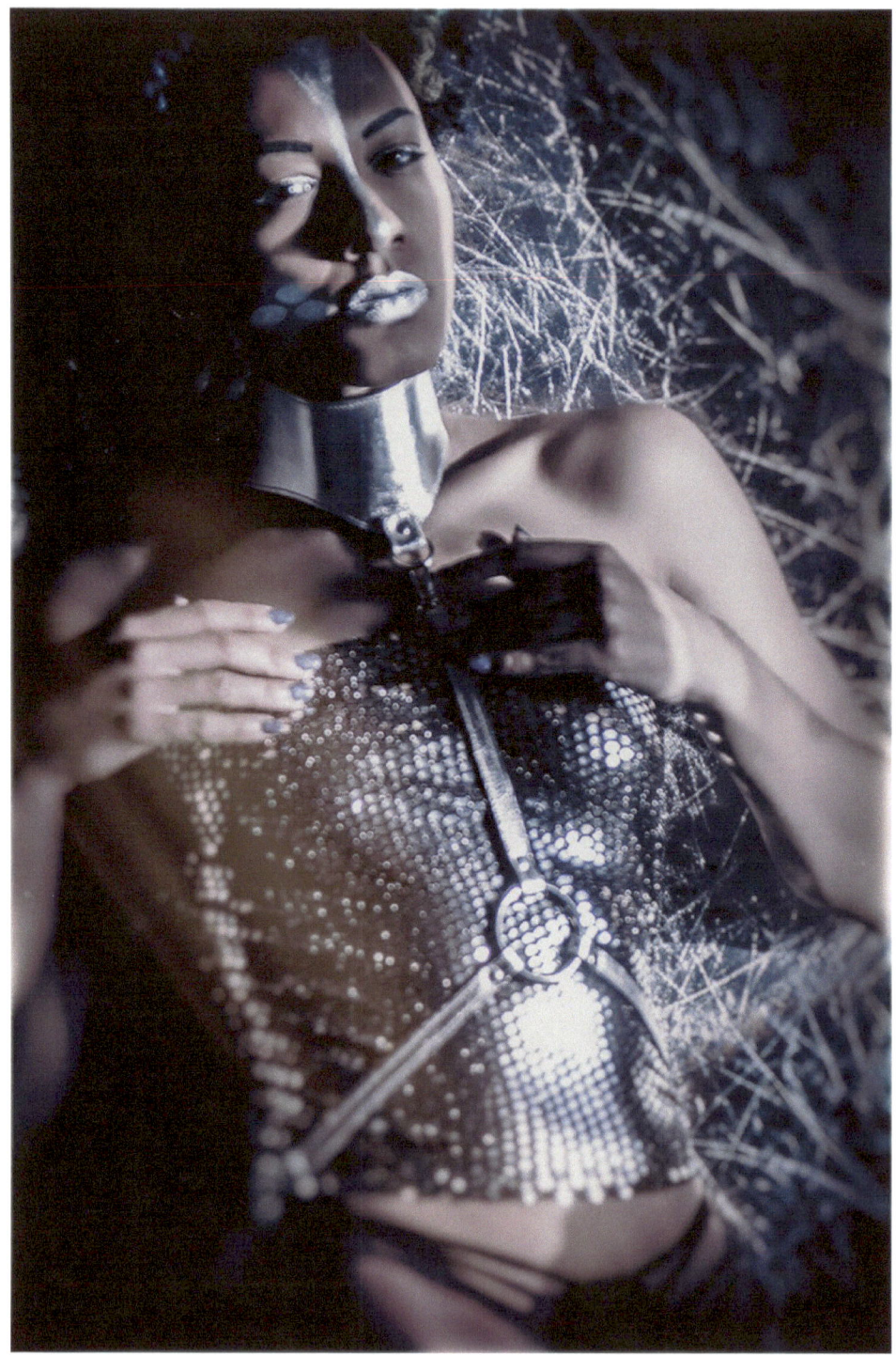

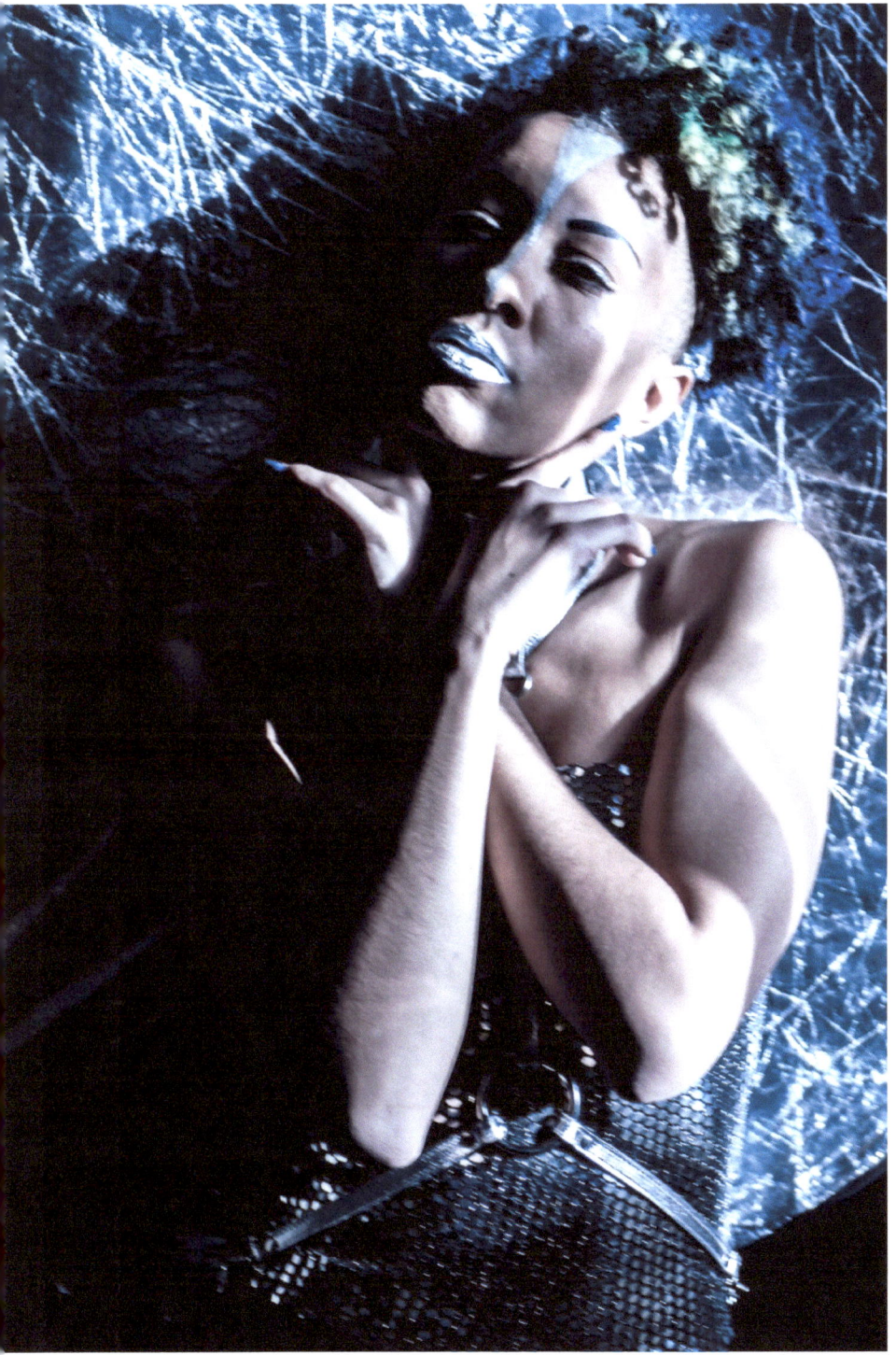

LOUD & QUEER

CW: None

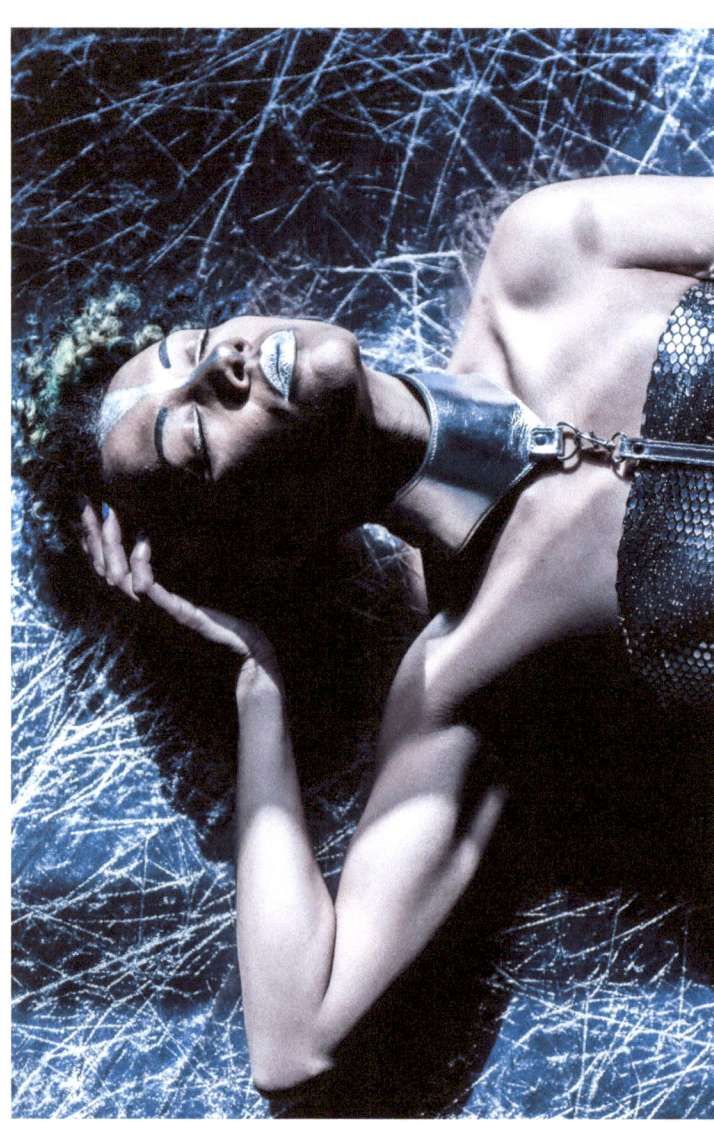

Aquarius (they/them) is an afrofuturist, non-binary queer artist & ambassador of living one's truth. Delivering their inimitable style of living art performance to the world – one stage, one dance floor, one mind at a time – Aquarius creates works that challenge, deconstruct and reimagine normative ideas of gender, race, and social politics. As the performative love-child of Grace Jones and Prince, and a child of vogue ballroom, they follow the footsteps of a rich legacy in gender performance and queer identity through the lens of the Black American experience.

Aquarius has reconnected with their true spirit through performance, embodying an identity that feels much more real than anything placed upon them before their creative awakening. They have built a practice of multi-disciplinary techniques, with performance at the core of each element. Their work dovetails with design, fashion, visual art and makeup artistry – ventures that Aquarius pursues with a passion. They create clothing, performance-wear, graphic visuals and designs that are the catalyst to their lifestyle vision, Get Funkked.
Read my manifesto here.

www.aquariusfunkk.com
getfunkked.wordpress.com
www.instagram.com/aquariusfunkk
www.vimeo.com/aquariusfunkk
paypal.me/aquariusfunkk
cash.app/shunkked

Chosen Family
Teddy Alexis Rodriguez

ACT ONE/TEASER
INT. RODRIGO'S APARTMENT - EARLY AFTERNOON
RODRIGO enters his apartment. He is a young professional. He is arriving from an interview. RODRIGO is in his 30s, he is an upbeat Afro-Latinx cis-gender gay male. The apartment is in very good shape. The furniture is missed-matched. The apartment has a very home-y feeling. RODRIGO is carrying a lot of groceries.
RODRIGO
Lana! Lana, I am home!
The sounds of loud lesbian sex are heard.
RODRIGO
God, I hope that's porn. Lana!?
LANA, an African-American woman, comes rushing into the room followed by Carolynn, a White woman.
LANA
Rodrigo, hi! You are a little early.
RODRIGO
I am actually an hour late, I told you I was coming in at 4pm. How are you Sherilynn?
CAROLYNN
It's Carolynn, sorry about the intrusion. I'll show myself out.
RODRIGO
No worries dear. Do you have a change of clothes? Stay for party. I can use another host!
CAROLYNN
(To LANA)
Is that okay?
LANA
Suuure. Go get your clothes.
CAROLYNN
No need! They are already in your room.
CAROLYNN exits.
LANA
Are you serious?

RODRIGO
Sorry I panicked! She not only looks exactly like Sherilynn, and what in the actual fuck her name is basically the same.

LANA
I have a type, what can I say?

RODRIGO
Please help me with the appetizers, people will be here any second. Your are messy.

LANA
Girl, be quiet!

ACT TWO
INT. RODRIGO'S APARTMENT - LATER THE SAME AFTERNOON
We see Rodrigo's living room ready to entertain. There are dips, salsas, crackers and chips everywhere. All of it has been personally done by Rodrigo, and he will let everyone know that he did. The bell rings. INGNACIO and ALBERTO enter. INGNACIO is a very confident man; he has a key to the apartment. ALBERTO is a meek/nerd man trying to be cool.

INGNACIO
Hello everyone! Where is everyone?

ALBERTO
Knowing Rodrigo, he probably told you the start time was an hour earlier, so you'd be on time. Since we are half an hour late, that really means that we are half an hour early, according to my assessment.

INGNACIO
That bitch! Oh no Alberto, Rodrigo made guacamole too.

ALBERTO
Dang it! He is going to steal the spotlight of my creamy guac!

RODRIGO enters.

RODRIGO
Hello guys! You guys are early.

ALBERTO
You told us the party started at 6:00pm.

INGNACIO
Yeah bitch. Where is everyone?

RODRIGO
Oh, I tricked you guys into being early. Good job Rodrigo from the past!
RODRIGO pads himself in the back.
INGNACIO
Is that boy you like coming?
RODRIGO
Austin? He sure is, but please he does not know I like him. So, please be discreet, and Alberto, please just do not talk to him. You always break.
ALBERTO
Yes, you are right! If I talk to him and there is a pause. I will say: so, Rodrigo is in love with you!
RODRIGO
(To INGNACIO)
It is your job to keep this queen away from my man.
Bell rings.
RODRIGO
Can you get that?
INGNACIO
Sure.
ROSIE enters. ROSIE, a Trans Woman, enters. She is accompanied with AUSTIN, who is the twinkle in RODRIGO's eye. AUSTIN, is a young LATINX man who is barely out of the closet.
ROSIE
(Coming in.)
Hello everyone.
INGNACIO
Can we help you?
ROSIE
Hello Ignacio! This is Austin.
INGNACIO
(Flirty.)
Hello there! And your name?
ROSIE
Rosie.
INGNACIO
I can't place you.
ROSIE
I was here for the Miss Universe party... we kinda hooked up?

INGNACIO
Juanito!?
ROSIE
(Cooly.)
I, obviously, don't go by that name
anymore.
RODRIGO
Ignacio, do you want to finish these
up? Please.
RODRIGO goes to the door area to say hi to the new arrivals.
RODRIGO
(Under his breath and to INGNACIO)
We can de-compress that later.
(To ROSIE and AUSTIN)
Hello guys. Austin, looking great.
AUSTIN
I brought some wine. I did not know
what to bring.
RODRIGO
Wine is always a winner! You guys can
have a seat.
ROSIE
(going to hug RODRIGO)
Hey honey! I missed you so much!
RODRIGO
I missed you too! Next trip to Texas,
I go with you!
ROSIE
(To RODRIGO)
I brought Austin for you. Yes, he is
single!
RODRIGO
Ok, we will see how the night goes.
RODRIGO
(to both AUSTIN and ROSIE)
If you guys want to eat, go ahead and
dig in. I made ALL of the food.
ALBERTO tries to get to ROSIE and AUSTIN.
RODRIGO
(To ALBERTO)
Excuse me sir, where are you going?
ALBERTO
To hang with Rosie.

RODRIGO
I do not think so. Ignacio! You need
Alberto to help you, don't you?
RODRIGO walks ALBERTO to INGNACIO.
RODRIGO
(To INGNACIO)
Do your job, this is going to be a
complicated night already. I do not
need Alberto free-ranging.
CAROLYNN and LANA enter. They are both looking great and
fresh.
LANA
Hi everyone!
INGNACIO & ALBERTO
(excited)
Sherilynn!
RODRIGO
Carolynn you guys!
INGNACIO and ALBERTO are so confused.
RODRIGO (CONT'D)
(To Carolynn)
Sorry, these dudes barely know any
White people. They are a little slow.
INGNACIO
(To Rodrigo)
What the fuck!?
RODRIGO
Just get with the program. Lana is
being messy as fuck.
LANA
So, Rodrigo, is that cute guy you like
coming? What's his name Austin?
RODRIGO knocks over the guacamole and falls.
INGNACIO
H i s n a m e i s n o t A u s t i n , h e I S f r o m
Austin.
ALBERTO
(To INGNACIO, under his breath)
Good save.
RODRIGO
(Standing up)
Anybody hungry? I made all the food.

LOUD & QUEER   CW: Explicit and Sexual Language

ACT THREE
INT. RODRIGO'S APARTMENT - LATER THAT EVENING
It is a little later at RODRIGO's party. The night is almost wrapping up and RODRIGO has not been able to get his moves on AUSTIN. RODRIGO is hanging out with ROSIE, LANA and CAROLYNN, while AUSTIN is with INGNACIO. ALBERTO stands awkwardly comparing and discussing the two guacamoles, by himself.

ROSIE
Rodrigo, have you even talked to Austin?

RODRIGO
I have been trying, but I have been busy hosting. I also have been avoiding it.

CAROLYNN
Why?

LANA
You think he is too hot for you.

RODRIGO
Well, he is ten years younger. It might as well be thirty years in gaytime.

ROSIE
You are one of the coolest guys I know. He would be lucky to have you.

RODRIGO
Thank you for the reference. I will submit it with my application.

LANA
...and you better submit that application before the committee closes the opening.

RODRIGO
What do you mean?

LANA
(pointing at INGNACIO)
That if you do not hurry, someone else will put IN an application.

INGNACIO and AUSTIN look very cozy as INGNACIO put his hand on AUSTIN's shoulder.

RODRIGO
Ignacio! Alberto needs help with the appetizers.

ALBERTO is completely un-phased and on his phone.

RODRIGO
(walking towards AUSTIN)
How is it going? Do you need another
drink?
RODRIGO grabs INGNACIO and gently leads him away from the
conversation.
AUSTIN
No, I am good. You threw a lovely get
together.
RODRIGO
I wanted to connect with you. I have
been running around like crazy, you
know, hosting.
AUSTIN
I wanted to connect with you too.
RODRIGO
Really? You know all of the food and
drinks were made by me.
AUSTIN
Yes. I hope I am not too forward, but
I was wondering...
Doorbell rings.
RODRIGO
That is probably the neighbors, they
get mad when brown people are having
fun. Please hold that thought.
RODRIGO goes to answer the door. We discover GEOFFREY, a very
handsome and very young man. GEOFFREY is RODRIGO's protégé.
GEOFFREY
(as he plants a huge kiss on
RODRIGO's mouth)
Hello everyone!
RODRIGO
This is Geoffrey everyone. Let me
introduce you, this Austin and you
know Ignacio and Alberto, and this is
Rosie and you know Lana and this is...
GEOFFREY
Sherilynn!
CAROLYNN
Carolynn.
GEOFFREY
Tomato/Tomato.
GEOFFREY mouths "I HATE YOU" to LANA.

LOUD & QUEER   CW: Explicit and Sexual Language

RODRIGO
Great, come Geoffrey, let me get you a drink.
GEOFFREY
Sounds lovely.
RODRIGO goes to the kitchen to prepare the drink. INGNACIO and ALBERTO are bored with the lack-luster of the party.
INGNACIO
How is the host doing?
RODRIGO
I am doing okay. Of course, Lana is not helping me at all and she is being so messy.
ALBERTO
Austin is by himself.
INGNACIO
I'll entertain him.
RODRIGO
Back off you bitch!
INGNACIO
What?
RODRIGO
Ignacio, I am not in the mood for your games. Please, pour a drink for Geoffrey and keep him away from Carolynn.
INGNACIO
Can I just hang with Austin? He seems more like my demographic.
RODRIGO
What the hell! He is AT LEAST ten years younger than you and I already bro-coded that when you got here.
INGNACIO
Whatever! Keep your man warm, he is looking like Alaska over there.
RODRIGO
Take this drink to Geoffrey please.
INGNACIO
Great, I get to hang with the "hetero" cock-tease of the year.
RODRIGO
Alberto, you keep an eye on him.
ALBERTO
I can't I am guarding the guac.

RODRIGO
That's my guac, not yours.
ALBERTO
I know, but most people like yours better, so I am just pretending I made it.
RODRIGO
OK?
RODRIGO goes to AUSTIN. He brings him a fresh drink.
RODRIGO
Here you go!
AUSTIN
Thank you so much! Good timing too.
RODRIGO
Sorry about the interruption.
AUSTIN
No worries. Thank you for the invite by the way.
RODRIGO
Of course! I am so happy to have you.
There is an awkward silent moment.
RODRIGO
I wanted to tell you that if you were inclined, and you do not have to feel pressured on this...
Doorbell rings.
RODRIGO
Are you kidding me!
AUSTIN
Are you still expecting more people?
RODRIGO
I do not. I will be right back. I am so sorry.
RODRIGO goes to the door and we discover SHERILYNN. SHERILYNN is LANA's girlfriend or ex-girlfriend, we are not sure at this moment. RODRIGO is so surprised by this, and he understands that if SHERILYNN comes in, it will be the end of the party.
RODRIGO
Sherilynn!
SHERILYNN
Hi Rodrigo! Are you having a party?
RODRIGO
(as he blocks the door)
Yes, I am.

SHERILYNN
I just want to talk to Lana. It is an emergency.
RODRIGO
I do not mean to be rude, but it will be best if you do not come in. I do not want to interrupt the party. You know how these things are.
SHERILYNN
Oh, of course! I will wait out here.
RODRIGO watches SHERILYNN leave and closes the door.
RODRIGO
(screams)
LANA!!!!
LANA
Sup, bro?
RODRIGO
Come here please.
LANA
What?
RODRIGO
Sherilynn is here.
LANA
What? Where?
RODRIGO
Outside. Please, I do not need this right now.
LANA
What don't you need?
RODRIGO
Your messiness.
LANA
What can I say? My honey drives them crazy.
RODRIGO
Get rid of Sherilynn. Now!
LANA goes to find SHERILYNN. RODRIGO rushes to AUSTIN.
RODRIGO
Just another day in paradise.
AUSTIN
What is going on?
RODRIGO
Two words: Lesbian Dra-ma.
AUSTIN
I get you.

RODRIGO
Do you need another drink?
AUSTIN
I'm good. Do you think it is time to
have that convo?
A loud argument is heard through the walls. It is clearly
SHERILYNN and LANA.
RODRIGO
(trying really hard to ignore the
fight)
Now will be a great time...
AUSTIN
...are those your friends?
RODRIGO
No, that is just the neighbor's TV,
they are watching Game of Thrones or
something.
AUSTIN
Are you sure?
RODRIGO
Yes, let me ask you this...
The fight gets louder.
AUSTIN
Should you check on your friends?
RODRIGO
They are okay.
AUSTIN
I wanted to ask you if Ignacio is
single because maybe you can talk to
him for me. He is so hot, but a guy
you can take home too you know?
RODRIGO
(screaming)
Are you fucking serious?
A thud from outside is done. RODRIGO goes to the door.
RODRIGO
Oh dear.
AUSTIN
Wait! Where are you going?
RODRIGO
(very mad)
I have to check on these bitches,
don't I?
LANA and SHERILYNN come into the room screaming.

LANA
How is this my fault?
SHERILYNN
How is it NOT your fault!
LANA
Yes. Just go home Sherilynn!
SHERILYNN
You were the one that texted me last night!
RODRIGO
Guys! Can you take this to Lana's room perhaps? Or do you want us to participate?
INGNACIO
That is a great idea.
CAROLYNN
Should I get involved in this?
RODRIGO
How about no?
SHERILYNN
W h y w o u l d y o u g e t i n v o l v e d ?
RODRIGO
Lana, take it to your room. Please!
LANA and SHERILYNN go to their room.
ROSIE
Well, I think this is the end of this party.
RODRIGO
Rosie, can you take Carolynn home please?
ROSIE
Sure. Where do you live?
CAROLYNN
Sure, maybe I should check on Lana?
ROSIE
It is not the best time. Let's go.
AUSTIN
Ok.
ROSIE
Austin, grab my plate. Please.
RODRIGO
(to Rosie)
Thanks babe. I am so sorry.
ROSIE

No worries, I have to deal with a
share of drama myself.
AUSTIN waves to RODRIGO, RODRIGO responds awkwardly to the
wave. ROSIE, AUSTIN and CAROLYNN leave.
ALBERTO
Well, that was fun!
RODRIGO
Fuck you, help me clean up.
INGNACIO
What happened with Austin?
RODRIGO
He asked me if you were single.
ALBERTO
Kiss of death.
RODRIGO
Exactly.
INGNACIO
I guess I win, again.
RODRIGO
Yes. You do.
ACT FOUR
INT. RODRIGO'S APARTMENT - SAME DAY LATE NIGHT
RODRIGO goes into the living room to grab a cup of water. He
is startled to see GEOFFREY crashing in the sofa.
RODRIGO
GEOFFREY!! What in gay hell?
GEOFFREY
Sorry, bro! I didn't mean to scare
you!
RODRIGO
What are you doing here, honey?
GEOFFREY
Lana told me I could stay? I was
kicked out of my apartment.
RODRIGO
Geoffrey! You are a mess babe.
GEOFFREY
Were you able to lock it down with
Austin?
RODRIGO
No, he likes Ignacio instead.
GEOFFREY
You can do better. No worries, bro.
Besides, Austin asked me out too!

RODRIGO
What?! That bitch.
GEOFFREY goes to RODRIGO and gives him a hug.
GEOFFREY
It's okay.
The hug continues.
RODRIGO
Oookay. Enough non-sexual contact.
Have a good night babe.
--The end--

About the author

Teddy was born in Ponce, PR. He is an LGBT+ Afro-Latinx independent scholar. He works devising inclusion in the arts.

Facebook @teddyalexisrodriguez Venmo @teddyalexis

Love
Milicent Fambrough

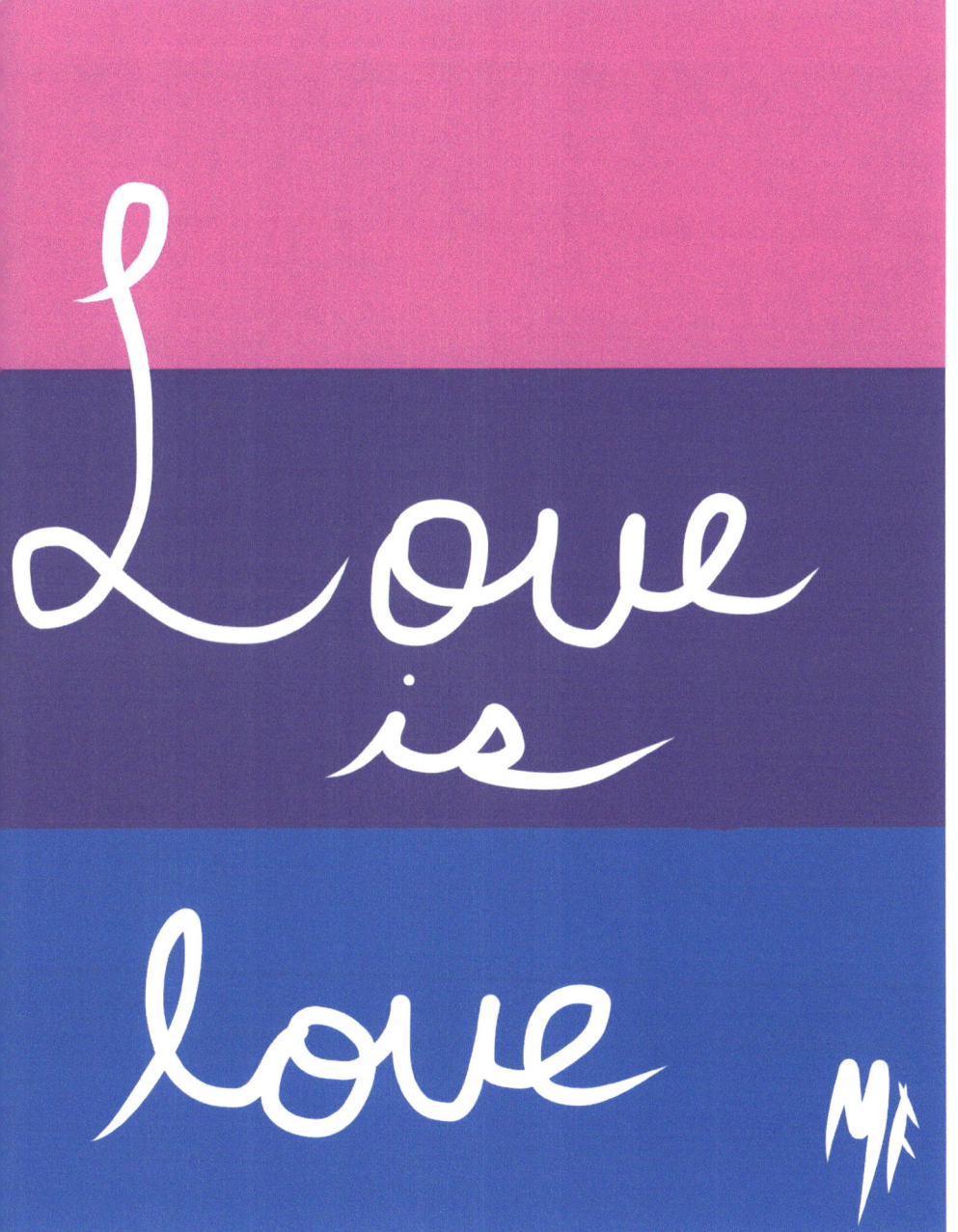

LOUD & QUEER   CW: None

Shape

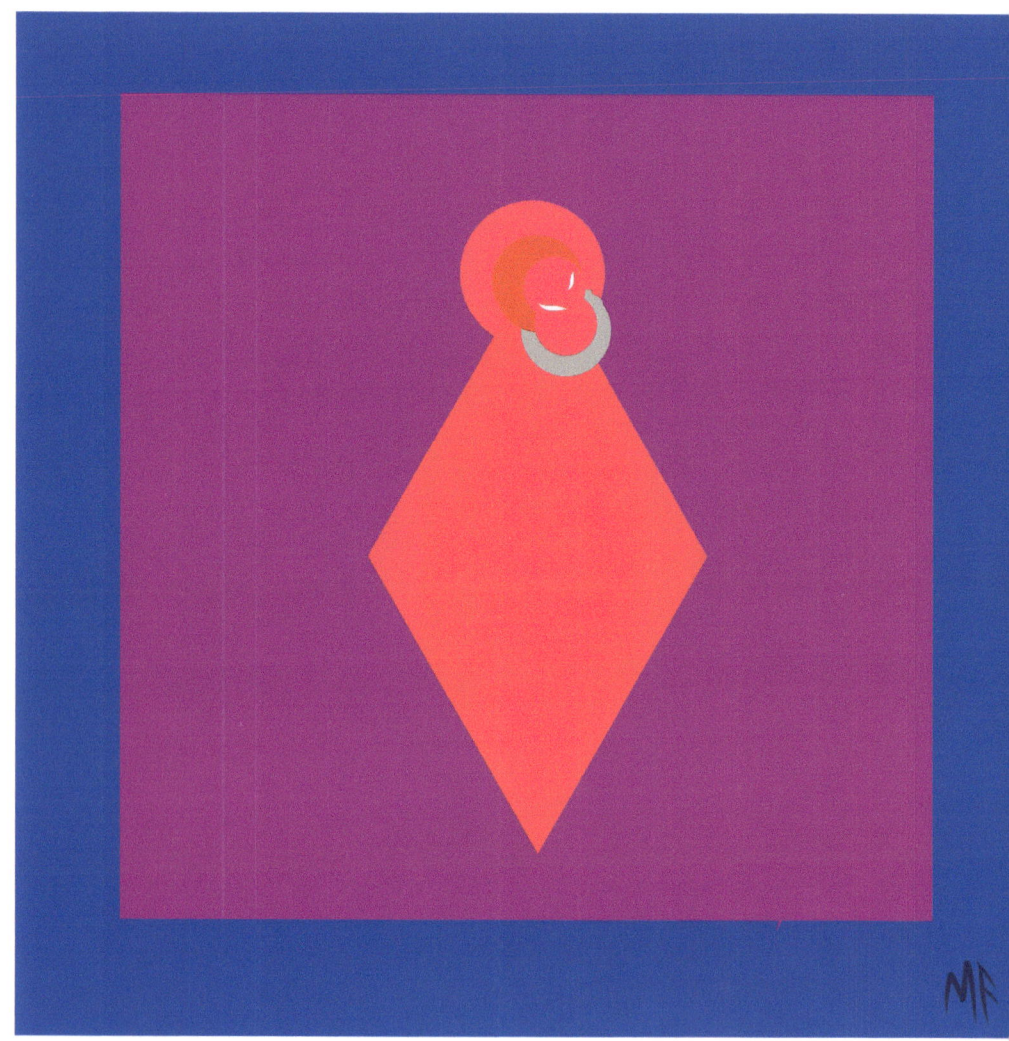

About the author

I am a contemporary artist and writer from San Antonio Texas. Currently focusing on cut paper artwork and writing poetry for publication.

Instagram handle @milicent210

New Intensity

It's funny how when you finally stop looking,
That's when all the things start to flow your way.
When you've finally surrendered is when the world says, "look it's okay",
and you breathe a sigh of relief and fill with excitement.

I had planned to turn my hatred for all things love related into a joke when he appeared.
He was so handsome, sweet and full of good intentions.
He smiled at me so genuine and we talked for eight whole hours.
My mind went blank and for the first time in a while; I was genuinely afraid.

And though I don't know where this is going,
I'd like to understand it in all it's intensity.
I've been dealt all the worst hands,
yet my heart tells me to run into this head first.
Throw all my cards down and see what happens,
I think I just might listen this time.

s.m

About the author:

Hello, my name is Spencer Millington. I am a twenty year old bisexual mixed black androgynous woman. These are three poems I selected from my collection entitled Tides, Sunflowers and New Intensity. I have been writing poetry for about five years on and off now and it is a major passion of mine. If anyone would like to read more of my work I have a small poetry account that I plan to be more active on called @idecidedtospeaktothetrees_ though my work tends to be heavy so I don't recommend it for people who don't enjoy reading sad writing.

Madoodle
Dr. Elijah Nicholas

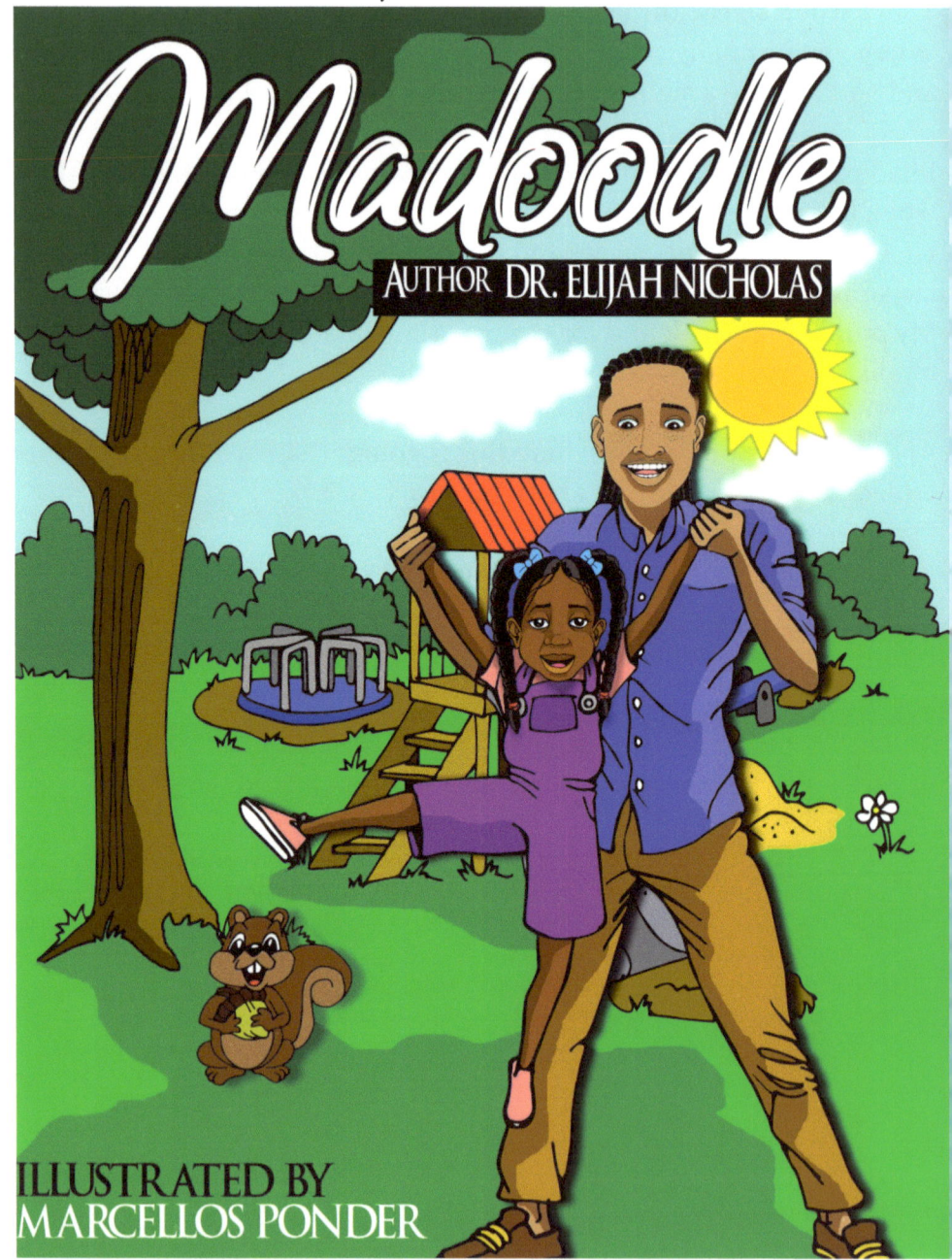

Madoodle

Dr. Elijah Nicholas has created an LGBTQI-friendly children's book featuring Madoodle (aka Madison), a ten-year-old girl whose Uncle Pete was once her Auntie Mary. Based on Dr. Elijah's personal experiences with family and friends as he navigated his gender transition from female to male, Dr. Elijah has brilliantly created a story of love, family, compassion, and an authentic gender expression acceptance. Through the eyes of Madoodle and her friends, with appearances by parents, teachers, and other bright and inquisitive children, Dr. Elijah entertains, educates, enlightens, and most of all contributes to the discussion of gender expression. Dr. Elijah recently retired as a Lt. Colonel after 24+ years in the US military. He served in the military well before experiencing his gender transition. Madoodle is certainly a tool, and example, for compassionate and loving family discussions, classroom lessons, and enlightening storytelling.

About the author:
Assigned the female gender at birth, Dr. Elijah Nicholas spent over half of his life in the US Military retiring as a senior officer in 2012. Transitioning from female-to-male in 2018 came as a result of Dr. Elijah no longer being able to live his core values: Authenticity, Integrity, and Transparency. After retiring from the military and then leading ministers and pastors around the globe, Dr. Elijah found it most befitting to resign his duties as a pastoral leader in 2018, just before he began his gender reassignment.

Since the onset of Dr. Elijah's gender transition, he has mentored individuals to remembering their true identity and living a full life. Dr. Elijah also guides organizations in helping to identify how authentic living impacts the individual and collective society. O
ne way Dr. Elijah helps individuals live their most authentic life is through his writings. His memoir, "Didn't Ask, Didn't Tell: The Life of A Gay Christian Soldier" chronicles Dr. Elijah's life as a girl who experienced sexual trauma, growing up in the African-American community where secrets were often the norm, and then living life as a lesbian for almost 25 years before retiring from the US Military. While Dr. Elijah was extremely pleased and freed by the self-publication of his memoir, he continued to live with a deeply rooted secret.

Ultimately, he could no longer navigatelife living as a female as he continued to expand his conscious. Subsequently, transitioning to Elijah Nicholas Meredith in 2018 was the saving grace for Dr. Elijah, literally. Transitioning and living life openly and authentically saved Dr. Elijah's life. Dr. Elijah has been a bridge for various communities seeking to understand the LGBTQI experience. Dr. Elijah helps expand the community experience through his most recent work, "Madoodle," a Children & Family fiction series that navigates unconditional love and gender expression. In this writing, Dr. Elijah aims to enlighten society while expanding the social constructs that sometimes restrict individuals from living their highest and trustiest self.

Dr. Elijah is now positioned as an multi-published Author, Community Advocate, Inspirational Speaker, and Spiritual Guide. Dr. Elijah holds a Doctorate in Business Administration from the University of Phoenix, a Masters in Business Administration, a Masters in Adult Education & Training, a Masters in Military Operational Art & Leadership, and a Bachelors of Science in Administration of Justice. A former pastor,
Dr. Elijah is also a licensed and ordained minister, leading Dr. Elijah Nicholas Ministries. He resides in Atlanta with his two amazing Boxers; Duke & Zeus.

SUPPORT
LOUD & QUEER
NOW & FOREVER

LOUD & QUEER is committed to giving a voice to the queer community and projecting those perspectives into the wider community. We want everyone to hear queer voices of now, and that is why our zine is given out freely to all that want to read it.

We rely on patrons and donations to keep the zine going. Did you love this issue? Want new issues of LOUD & QUEER in the future? Want to receive exclusive perks and rewards while supporting LGBTQIA+ creators?

Become a patron of LOUD & QUEER

PATREON.COM/LOUDANDQUEERZINE

BLACK LIVES MATTER Special Ezine   August 2020

©LOUD & QUEER 2020   Marisa Wohlschlaeger

www.ingramcontent.com/pod-product-compliance
Lightning Source LLC
Chambersburg PA
CBHW040330220526
45473CB00009B/2634